YE MUST BE BORN AGAIN

SAYS THE MASTER

THOMAS J. MURPHY

DEDICATION & ACKNOWLEDGEMENTS

All Glory to God the Father,
God the Son & God the Holy Ghost.

Special thanks to Jamie Rice and Pam Terrell for
their compilation and input to Chapters 1 & 2;
indebtedness to Wendy Bowen for her
precision-like editing and instruction on wording
and syntax as well as process-education for
developing as an author.

Tell Giff, "I'll see him on the morrow.".

CONTENTS

CHAPTER 1
INITIAL THOUGHTS

The title to this book, of course, comes from John 3:7 in the New Testament in which Jesus declares to Nicodemus, a very upstanding man in Jewish Society, the requirement to enter into heaven. Jesus' simple, straight-forward response to Nicodemus' curiosity caught Nicodemus off-guard, which was apparent by his misunderstanding of Jesus' profound statement. Nicodemus could only comprehend it from a natural standpoint, "Can a man enter into his mother's womb a second time?" Obviously, this is a physical impossibility, but that's all he had to go by in his reservoir of mental perception. Jesus was speaking of another realm: the unseen realm, which is not seen in the natural but is seen in the spirit.

From the original Greek text, *born again* is *gennao anothen* which means to be born or begotten from above or anew or again. This speaks of a spiritual transaction: a reality, not a theoretical belief or change of habit or attitude even though these can be and should be a result of the "born-again" experience. It implies that a fresh dynamism takes place from a non-natural or supernatural source. This is why it is a shocking statement, an affront to the natural man, because it utterly disables the idea of any logical or rational processes to ensure a safe passage into eternity. The Apostle Paul said, "The natural man receiveth not the things of the spirit for they are foolishness unto Him, neither can he know them, because they are spiritually discerned." (1 Cor 2:14.) As the old saying goes, "It is better felt than telt, caught than taught," meaning that one must experience it for themself.

This is the main reason it is so difficult to communicate the truth of the reality of the born-again experience to humanity. Unless someone has truly experienced it, they cannot fully explain it. Personally, I grew up playing football for a predominant portion of my formative years and, in conversations with others of my peer group, I could easily differentiate the real football players from the "wannabes." The look in their eyes and their tone of voice distinguished their reality or talk thereof, and the level of enthusiasm was often the tell-tale sign. When something or someone is real to you, there is an innate desire to express it to others in some form, even if one does not consider himself or herself a communicator. Real communication is much more than words, though words are important.

The greatest experience that one can communicate in human life is that of love. This is the basis of the born-again experience: God's love for each and every person conceived in the womb. It's wonderful to know John 3:16 by heart, "For God so loved the world, that he gave his only begotten son, that whosoever believeth in him should not perish but have everlasting life." However, it's an even greater epiphany to understand that God loves you personally. Think about that: out of all the billions of people that have been born throughout the ages, He knows and loves you personally. King David testified, "My substance was not hid from thee, when I was made in secret, and curiously wrought in the lower parts of the earth. Thine eyes did see my substance, yet being imperfect, and in thy book all my members were fashioned when as yet there was none of them." (Ps. 139:15-16.) What an awesome truth to ponder! The God of heaven and earth knew you and formed you in the womb! His love is beyond measure or comprehension, and absolutely puts to naught the vaulted intellect-ualism, the elitism, the syncretism, and the pride of this world. God's love was and is so great for mankind in its sinful state that He sent the most precious treasure in the universe to the world: His Beloved Son, the pure, sinless, matchless, blessed Son of God! Apostle Paul states, "while we were sinners, Christ died for us" (Rom. 5:8.) This is truly unconditional love: love given when nothing is expected in return. Jesus said, "Greater love hath no man than this, that a man lay down his life for his friends" (Jn. 15:13.) Amen and amen!

This is the primary need of the human heart, not the physical but the spiritual. If you know that you are loved and can return love back, then you have a sense of fulfillment and destiny in life. The famous verse in 1 Corinthians 13, often quoted in wedding ceremonies, "...Now abideth faith, hope, love [charity in KJV] these three, but the greatest of these is love" is an undeniable truth. It is the motivation for everything God does, even sending His pure, sinless, pristine son to a sin-sick world to die for the sins of mankind so that we would have a way to be with God in eternity. Dottie Rambo penned this song that captures the message of God's love very well:

Song: If That Isn't Love...
*He left the splendor of Heaven
Knowing His destiny
Was the lonely hill of Golgotha
To lay down His life for me.
Chorus:
If that isn't love, then the ocean is dry
There's no stars in the sky
And the sparrow can't fly
If that isn't love.
Then Heaven's a myth
There's no feeling like this,
If that isn't love
Even in death, He remembered
The thief hanging by His side
And He spoke of love and compassion
Then He took Him to paradise
(Chorus)*

Elvis Presley recorded this song in 1974, and if you can listen to him sing this song and are not touched, then your wood is wet, you may need a heart check. How high, how wide, how deep is the love of God. But His love alone is not enough to save

4

anyone. It makes the provision for salvation and grants us the right to be born again. Ephesians 2:8-9, "By grace are ye saved through faith; and that not of yourselves: it is the gift of God: not of works, lest any man should boast." Notice: by grace, not by love are you saved. G.R.A.C.E. means God's Riches At Christ's Expense. Grace comes from the Greek word *charis*, meaning the divine influence upon a soul and the reflection of it in one's life. In essence, for grace to take effect in its reality, there must be a **receiving** of it as well. John 1:12 says, "But as many as received him, to them gave he power [the right] to become the sons of God, even to them that believe on his name." Then John 1:13 establishes the basis of the born-again reality, though he does not use the expression itself, "...which were born not of blood, nor of the will of flesh, nor of the will of man, but of God." It is a spiritual birth. This is what lends credence to that old saying, "Born once, die twice; born twice, die once." A sobering but awesome truth. If all you have in this life is a physical birth, then you not only go through a physical death, but also a spiritual death according to Revelation 20:14-15, a most surreal moment. However, if you are not only here by being born in the natural but have been through a spiritual birth by being born again, then the second death has no power over you because of the life of God in you; thus, you only die physically.

The Bible is very clear on life, death, the judgment to come, heaven, hell, and eternity. It makes no place for ambiguity on critical issues of true reality. Purgatory, or the belief that there's a holding place after death for those whose judgment is still hangs in the balance, is a doctrine of man that was developed to soften and marginalize the sovereign rule and righteous execution of God's preordained laws of the universe and eternity. You are either a child of God through the born-again experience or you are not. This feel-good bromide that states, "we are all children of God" is a potentially dangerous misnomer which can ultimately lead men and women to hell. Yes, we are all God's creation, and He loves His creation, but He qualifies the sonship relationship only for those who have been born again. "For ye are all the children of God by faith in Christ Jesus" (Gal. 3:26.) Jesus said, "This is life eternal, that they might know thee, the only true God and Jesus Christ whom thou hast sent" (Jn. 17:3.) The word for *know* in the Greek, is *ginosko*, which means an intimate knowledge, and is something much deeper than intellectual understanding. Even as Adam *knew* his wife and she conceived a child. God imparts Himself into man's spirit to produce the born-again result and thus, a man, woman or child truly knows God as their Father and Jesus Christ as their Savior. Notice how clear and concise Jesus' statement is regarding eternal life: "This is...", not "This could be" or "This should be" or "This has great importance" or "is strongly recommended." No, He says in no uncertain terms, without exception, what eternal life is. Jesus says in Matthew 7:14, "...strait is the gate and narrow is the way which leadeth unto life, and few there be that find it." The word *life* is the Greek word *zoe*, which, in essence, is the God kind of life as opposed to the natural life of our mind, will, intellect, and emotions as it relates to the physical world around us through our five senses: taste, touch, sight, hearing, and smelling. Until the Holy Spirit imparts *zoe* into one's being, they do not have the life of God in their inner man.

Man is a tri-part-being: spirit, soul and body (Greek: *pneuma, psuche,* and *soma*.) Before one comes to God, the spirit man is dead to God. This is why the Apostle Paul says in Ephesians 2:1, "And you hath he quickened, who were dead in trespasses and sins." This is why man must be born again. Man is alive to the natural world, but dead to his Creator as their Father. Man needs to have a spiritual birth to enter into the heavenly realm and appropriate God as his Father. The Lord said, "No man cometh to the Father, but by me" (Jn. 14:6.) You may have heard a preacher say at one time or another, "No man cometh to God but by Jesus Christ." Actually, we will all come to God. To clarify this, according to Romans 14:12: "So then every one of us shall give account of himself to God [in the final judgment.]" Hebrews 10:31 says, "It is a fearful thing to fall into the hands of the living God." But to come to God as your loving Heavenly Father, you must come by Jesus Christ as your Savior.

He is the only Savior in the history of the world. All others that claim to be great spiritual or religious leaders (i.e., Mohammed, Buddha, Joseph Smith, Sun Young Moon, etc.) were all just mere men in comparison while Jesus Christ was and is God Almighty in the flesh who lived a perfect, sinless life as a man which qualified Him to be the Sinless Savior. No one else could die for our sins and reconcile us to a holy God but Him. "And lo, a voice came from heaven, saying, 'This is my beloved Son in whom I am well pleased.'" (Matt. 3:17.) Job 9:33 records, "Neither is there a daysman [umpire] betwixt us [God and Job] that might lay his hand upon us both." Job knew he needed a mediator between a holy God and himself to reconcile a ruptured relationship. Job believed that God would send a redeemer in the fulness of time to effect this. Job confirmed this in Job 19:25, "For I know that my redeemer liveth and that he shall stand at the latter day upon the earth."

Hopefully, this first chapter lays down a foundation for the thesis of this book and the reality that it opens up for us. The bottom line is that we are all born with an inclination towards self-will. We just want to do what our natural man dictates to us with the influence of the world and the enemy of our souls, satan himself. We all must surrender our wills to the will of God so that He can direct our lives in the way that He would have us to go. You must admit you are a sinner and ask Christ to save you from eternal damnation and also from yourself! This is how you become born again. Romans 10:9-10 says, "That if thou shalt confess with thy mouth the Lord Jesus and shalt believe in thine heart that God hath raised him from the dead, thou shalt be saved. For with the heart man believeth unto righteousness; and with the mouth confession is made unto salvation."

If you believe this with all your heart, pray this out loud: "God, save me from eternal separation from you and save me from my own way. I believe Jesus is Lord and I confess it with my mouth boldly. Thank you for doing it. Thank you for making me your child, in Jesus' name."

CHAPTER 2
THE NECESSITY OF IT

One may ask, of course, "What is all this fuss about being "born again?" It is a fair question. Why not just accept people the way they are and leave it at that? As human beings, certainly we accept others in the human family for who they are regardless of race, creed, color, national origin, or first language (at least we should accept everyone in this way.) However, God, being altogether holy, can only accept perfection into His kingdom. He is too pure to look on sin, and that is the key to understanding the necessity for the born-again experience.

S-I-N is the reason we, as fallen humans, absolutely need the new birth. We are all born in sin into this world according to the Bible, which is the Word of God. King David, one of the greatest men in the history of the world, said in Psalm 51:5-6, "Behold, I was shapen in iniquity and in sin did my mother conceive me. Behold, thou desirest truth in the inward parts and in the hidden part, thou shall make me know wisdom." David acknowledged the sin on the inside of him and the need for it to be replaced with God imparting truth and wisdom to his inner man.

The great Jonathan Edwards, the leader of The Great Awakening in the 1700s in colonial America, said in his epic sermon titled *Sinners in the Hands of an Angry God*, that "sin is the ruin and misery of the soul, it is destructive in its nature; and if God should leave it without restraint, there would need nothing else to make the soul perfectly miserable." Sen. Daniel Webster, one of America's greatest statesman ever, called Edwards the greatest American that ever lived. Edwards' words are certainly worthy of our attention, even nearly 300 years later.

Of course, if you understand that sin originated in the first family of the human race, it is easier to accept the ubiquity of sin and evil in the world. When Adam and Eve followed the bait of the serpent into eating the forbidden fruit, it utterly plunged mankind into a sink of depression, alienation from their Creator, and a powerful vortex of walking in self-determination, self-affection, and unbridled selfishness. The horrific consequences of Adam and Eve's fall in the Garden of Eden cannot be overstated. The root cause of all the ills and pains of the human experience can be traced back to sin within the individual, the family, the financial system, the political structure, national contentions, international conflicts, and even creation itself.

Sin produces death. In fact, Romans says that sin actually pays wages: "The wages of sin is death." (Rom. 6:23.) Sin is literally the cause of every problem that has ever existed on earth. Sickness, lack of

11

provision, poverty, promiscuity, powerlessness, hate, disharmony, racism, fascism, communism, decadence, death, destruction, despair, damnation, defeat, loss, licentiousness, divorce, conflict, war, selfishness, pride, impure passions, foul mouth, profanity, jealousy, envy, drunkenness, dope addiction, fetishes, witchcraft, variance, sex slavery, lying, cheating, deception, laziness, apathy, fear, unabridged anger, ignorance (of God), ungodliness, lovelessness, wastefulness, and many other pains of this life can be traced back to sin.

Mark my words. Sin will take you further than you planned to go. It will cause you to stay longer than you ever thought, and it will cost you more time, money, heartache, pain, and trouble than your mind could ever imagine. It is the answer to why man suffers in this life, beyond all other explanations.

One of the most difficult aspects of sin is its ability to hide its real agenda. The Bible states that Moses "chose rather to suffer affliction with the people of God than to enjoy to pleasures of sin for a season" (Heb. 11:25.) Moses was unusual in that he was able to resist the easier path of sin. Sin can make itself look good, and since man is selfish at his core, sin can appear to be right. Proverbs 14:12 says, "There is a way which seemeth right unto a man, but the end thereof are the ways of death." Sin can look good, feel good, sound good, and taste good... until it doesn't. How many good marriages have been destroyed because the grass looked greener on the other side? One of the spouses in a marriage was lured away because of the siren song of more happiness with someone else. The devil is a liar, but he is slick at being one, and he uses the sin nature within us to pull us out of the path or person God has ordained for us (Matt. 19:6.) Jonathan Edwards said, "There are those corrupt principles in reigning power in them (carnal men) and in full possession of them, that are the seeds of hell-fire. These principles are active and powerful, exceeding violent in their nature...."[1] It is so ingrained in the human family that sin does not appear to be sin but the natural disposition of man and not some issue related to the fallen state of mankind. Sin is deceptive, diabolical and destructive. No human power can defeat it, overcome it, or subdue it. Yes, we can dress it up on the outside, turn over a new leaf as it were, and develop a better habit, all of which are good things, but the sin nature in the heart of man is still present. Only Christ can take away the inclination to sin out of our hearts. It takes more than a reformation; it takes a transformation. Only the born-again experience by the power of God can effectuate this.

Webster's dictionary defines sin in part as "a vitiated [impaired or weakened] state of human nature in which the self is estranged from God. From the Hebrew there are several words for *sin*, but the original word for it is initially used in Genesis 4:7 as God addresses Cain, *chatta* (#2403 in Strong's Concordance.) It generally speaks of "missing the mark" or an offense. Depending on context, it can also refer to a "sin-offering." In the New Testament

---

[1] From Four Classic Sermons by Warren Wiersbe

Greek, the word is *hamartia* (#266 in Strong's Concordance) and like the Hebrew, it means missing the mark, or an offense. 1 John 3:4, "for sin is the transgression of the law" states it without equivocation and as a matter of fact. The Amplified Bible translates the last portion of 1 John 3:4 like this: "For that is what sin is, lawlessness (the breaking and violating, of God's law by transgression or neglect, or being unrestrained and unregulated by His commands and his will.)"

We can see that by any definition, sin is not good. It causes the deterioration of the moral fiber of an individual, a family, a neighborhood, a town, a city, a state, a nation, a world. Like cancer, it spreads, metastasizes, destroys, decimates, damns, and inflicts suffering, pain, anguish, torment, alienation, sorrow, and a myriad of resulting consequences on the human family. This is all a result of the fall in the Garden of Eden with Adam and Eve. Of course, God held Adam responsible for the act of high treason with the serpent, satan's instrument to deceive Eve. This is why The Apostle states emphatically, "For as in Adam all die, so also in Christ shall all be made alive" (1 Cor. 15:22.)

We are all in Adam through physical birth, and just as we, the human family, inherit physical or natural attributes of our forefathers, we also, unfortunately, inherit the spiritual attributes, particularly the sin nature. Truly, it may manifest itself in different ways, whether it be alcohol addiction, drug addiction, anger issues, promiscuity, lust, jealousy, pride, or other harmful behavior, but it has the same root. That root is selfishness, a drive to bring about a desired end which our impulses, inclinations, and carnal contrivances dictate to us.

Romans 5:12 says, "Wherefore, as by one man sin entered into the world, and death by sin, and so death passed upon all men for that all have sinned." Sin is sin no matter the form of it, and it all brings forth the same result: death, most of all spiritual death, which in turn contributes to physical death. God told Adam in the Garden, warning him about the "tree of knowledge of good and evil, thou shall not eat of it: for in the day that thou eatest thereof, thou shalt surely die" (Gen. 2:17.)

Obviously, Adam and Eve did not die in the 24-hour day after they partook, but they did die in the prophetic day after their disobedience. Psalm 90, attributed to Moses, says in verse 4 that "a thousand years in thy sight are but as yesterday when it is past, and as a watch in the night." The Apostle Peter confirms this thought, saying "that one day is with the Lord as a thousand years, and a thousand years as one day." (2 Pet. 3:8.) Adam died at 930 years old, within the 1,000-year prophetic day God said he would. He died spiritually first through sin and then was cut short in his natural life.

The solemn, sobering, serious mess of sin cannot be expressed in words alone. The horrific, terrifying consequences that sin produces are immeasurable, catastrophic, and exceedingly sorrowful. We live in a moral universe and whether we like it or not is immaterial. God made the universe, and He gets to set the rules. Because this is so, there is a price to pay for rebellion against the Creator.

However, as much as He is a holy God, Isaiah records that He is a thrice holy God in Isaiah 6:2, He is also a God of love (1 John 4:8.) God was caught in a conundrum, so to speak, as He had to judge sin while at the same time wanting to save His creation from eternal separation from His presence. This, of course, is why He sent His Son to pay the price of redemption from the slave-market of sin because man had no way to claw his way back to fellowship after his fall in the Garden.

God promised a coming Messiah speaking to the serpent in the Garden, telling him "the seed of the woman would bruise his head" (Gen. 3:15) which is known as the *proto-evangelium*, the first declaration of the gospel referring to the virgin birth of the Messiah. Normal birth is typically referred to as the *seed of the man*, but God was already introducing a supernatural solution to the sin problem referring to the Holy Spirit's impregnation of a virgin named Mary several millennia down the line.

Sin could not be defeated by natural means, the seed of the man; this would be at best a stalemate with no winner. God's ace up his sleeve was His Son to take the place of sinners in order for God's holy wrath to be satisfied. This is how God solved the sin problem. For God to be just, He had to punish sin while His love nature compelled Him to act decisively. Romans 11:22 says, "Behold therefore the goodness and severity of God; on them which fell, severity, but toward thee, goodness, if thou continue in his goodness...." Oh, the riches and wisdom of the Eternal One! His ways are past finding out!

We can begin to understand the bottomless pit of the utter despicableness and ugliness of sin when we look at the indescribable horror of the sufferings of Christ in the torture and sacrifice of the cross. The prophet Isaiah speaks of the repulsiveness of the excruciating trauma the Messiah would suffer in Chapter 52: "As many were astonied at thee; his visage was so marred, more than any man, and his form more than the sons of men." Christ endured more pain than anyone else in history, as the physical agony revealed something much deeper and greater: the emotional and spiritual anguish beyond anything one could attempt to describe or communicate.

To truly understand the depth and depravity of sin, we must see by faith Christ on the cross in all its bloodstained gory. The Bible says, "For He [God the Father] made Him [God the Son] who knew no sin to be sin for us that we might be made the righteousness of God in him [Christ]" (2 Cor. 5:21.) On him, meaning Christ, fell severity, but we received goodness. This is known in theological circles as "The Great Exchange." "We owed a debt we could not pay; He paid a debt He did not owe. I needed someone to wash my sins away," as the old song goes (author is anonymous.)

We believe this to be the effect of the work of Jesus Christ on the cross of Calvary. We accept His sacrifice on the cross as totally efficacious, thorough, complete, and a fully paid debt to sin. "Jesus paid it all, all to him I owe; sin had left a crimson stain, He washes white as snow." (Written by Elvina Hall in 1865, music attributed to John Grape.)

Interestingly enough, the word *cross* is only mentioned 28 times in the New Testament though it is without controversy the central theme of the Christian faith. The cross is only mentioned in the Epistles by the Apostle Paul because though he was one who was "born out of due time," the Lord gave him "the message of the cross." The KJV uses the expression "the preaching of the cross" (1 Cor. 1:18) while the NKJV uses "the message of the cross," and the ESV says, "the word of the cross." From the Greek, *preaching* is the word *logos*, the expression of thought, an embodiment of conception, a treatise. Paul received this, the *message of the cross* (NKJV) as a revelation to the church and, ultimately, to the world.

Of all the achievements in the history of the world, the work of the cross completed by Christ is without equivocation the greatest ever. We could consider all the achievements of man: artistic, scientific, technological, educational, financial, relational, religious, athletic, academic, dramatic, leadership, motivational, journalistic, military, architectural, engineering, agricultural, environmental, maritime, aeronautic, space exploration, mountain conquering, thematic, inventions, and all other endeavors worthy of note, and they all pale in comparison to the work of the cross of Calvary. Christ has thoroughly and completely paid the full satisfactory compensation for all the debt of sin for all time and eternity and simultaneously defeated all the powers of darkness and evil, thereby making provision for total victory over sin and its effects.

The disconnect between the victory of the cross and the evil in the world today is God's timeline on His prophetic plan as well as man's blindness to God's strategic intervention in the affairs of man by way of the cross. The Apostle Paul speaking to the church at Corinth said, "But if the gospel be hid, it is hidden to them that are lost: In whom the god of this world hath blinded the minds of them which believe not, lest the light of the glorious gospel of Christ, who is the image of God, should shine unto them." (2 Cor. 4:3-4.) You could be awarded $10 million to your bank account, but if you are ignorant of it and never look at your statements, it does not benefit you. God sent the Savior to the world for all who would open their hearts to him and benefit from the preordained provision, planned from the foundation of the world.

Rest assured, the god of this world, the devil, does not want your eyes opened to God's divine solution to sin and its effect. The devil and his cohorts are on their way to hell in the lake of fire and are determined to take as many souls with them as they can. The devil's greatest weapon is deception. Dr. J. Vernon McGee used to say that we should be concerned about the devil as a serpent in the

Garden of Eden because he was more subtle than any other creature in the Garden. The word *subtle* in Hebrew is *arum*, meaning cunning, sly, or crafty. We should be more concerned with him as a dragon in the Book of Revelation from all the eating he has been doing with the dust of the earth because we are made of dust. But we should be most concerned with him as he is able to transform himself into an "angel of light." 2 Corinthians 11:14 says, "And no marvel; for Satan himself is transformed into an angel of light." His powers of deception are unsurpassed, and one of his greatest tools of deception is religion, deceiving the human family that by some systematic formation of religious rules, whatever form it may be, Eastern religion, Islam, or even Christian religion, through which people can indemnify themselves before the judgment bar of God. Paul clearly states in Galatians 2:16, "Knowing that a man is not justified by the works of the law, but by the faith of Jesus Christ, even we have believed in Jesus Christ, that we might be justified by the faith of Christ, and not by the works of the law: for by the works of the law shall no flesh be justified." Moreover he records in Romans 7:18, "For I know that in me, that is, in my flesh, dwelleth no good thing: for to will is present with me; but how to perform that which is good I find not." In other words, Paul is admitting that no matter how hard he tried, he could not keep all of the law. James 2:10 comments, "For whosoever shall keep the whole law, and yet offend in one point, he is guilty of all [of the law.]"

The law was given as a test, so to speak, to prove to

man that he could never live up to God's standards in his natural ability. In Galatians 3:24, Paul says, "Wherefore the law was our schoolmaster to bring us unto Christ, that we might be justified by faith." It has been said the salvation is "by grace alone through faith alone because of Christ alone." We could not overcome our sin nature in ourselves, so God sent His Son to undo the heavy burden of guilt because of this perpetual weakness which the enemy of our souls is always ready to take advantage of such. 1 John 3:8 testifies, "He that committeth sin is of the devil; for the devil sinneth from the beginning. For this purpose was the Son of God manifested that he might destroy the works of the devil." Praise God for the victory we have in Christ Jesus!!!

Christ, and Christ alone, can rectify you before a holy God. Christ is the answer for the world today, and He is the answer for each of us individually for whatever need we may have.

Perhaps the most significant chapter in the Bible pertaining to the fullness of the experience of the cross itself is Isaiah 53. Parenthetically speaking, it has been called the least read chapter in the synagogue because it so plainly prophesies the suffering fulfilled by Jesus on the cross. It graphically depicts the suffering Messiah in His mission, His selflessness, and complete obedience to the Father's will to appease the wrath of God against rebellion and reconcile lost mankind back to the Creator. The details of the suffering of Christ are astounding when you consider Isaiah penned this about 700 years before Jesus was born into this sin-sick world. Verses

3, 4, and 5 reverberate with telling accuracy and depth of feeling: "a man of sorrows and acquainted with grief," "borne our griefs and carried our sorrows," "stricken, smitten by God," "afflicted," "wounded for our transgressions [outward sins], bruised for our iniquities [(inward sins], by his stripes, we are healed." Such expressions can only grasp you and cause you to cry out for the Savior's mercy.

If you take it to heart, this all speaks to the remedy for sin and its effect. One must conclude if the remedy is so agonizing and exhaustive, what is the depth of depravity and hideousness of the cause? It must be immeasurable, an endless pit with no bottom. This is why man could not solve the sin problem in mankind. It took the God-man, Jesus Christ, to utterly decimate it at the cross to free us from the burden we carried throughout all the generations.

As we can see, sin in any form is debilitating, the source of all mankind's ills. It leads to despair, devastation, destruction, death, and damnation, but God's grace is greater than all our sin. Jesus condemned sin in the flesh to bring us new life free from the load of guilt and shame sin produces. Call upon him today and see if God doesn't show up in your life as a living reality. Pray this prayer with all your heart if you are so led and want Jesus to take over your life:

"God, I know I am a sinner. I need a Savior to redeem me from sin. I believe Jesus Christ is the true and living Savior and Lord. I humbly ask you, Lord, to wash my sins away with your blood and take over my life. Thank you for doing it. I ask all this in Jesus' name. Amen."

CHAPTER 3

THE BLOOD

I think it would be almost impossible to write any dissertation about salvation without featuring the blood of Christ. Hebrews 9:22 says, "Without the shedding of blood is no remission [of sins.]" It's difficult to understand from the human standpoint why the blood is so necessary to salvation or to make one born-again. Since sin brings forth death, there must be life to overcome death and that life is in the blood. Leviticus 17:11 says, "The life of the flesh is in the blood and I [God] have given it to you upon the altar to make atonement for the souls, for it is the blood that makes atonement for the soul." The word *atonement* from the Hebrew is *kaphar* (#3722 in Strong's Concordance) which means to appease or expiate or reconcile or cover. Interestingly, it is the same word that is translated *pitch* in Genesis when God told Noah to *pitch* the ark with bitumen; in a sense, the boat was *expiated* from God's wrath, the flooding of the world.

Of course, the blood of animal sacrifices of the Old Testament was not the same as the blood of Jesus. Hebrews 10:4 says, "For it is not possible that the blood of bulls and goats could take away sins." The

Levitical sacrificial system was established to atone for sins, not to remit them. The blood of Jesus Christ, when applied by faith, washes away sin never to be remembered again. John the Baptist, who was actually a cousin of Jesus, said upon seeing Jesus as He was about to enter into 3½ years of ministry, "Behold the Lamb of God which taketh away the sin of the world" (Jn. 1:29.) Jesus' blood was sinless, divine, pure, untainted blood from the eternal realm of heaven. The Apostle Peter said, "Forasmuch as ye know that ye were not redeemed with corruptible things, as silver and gold, from your vain conversation [way of life] received by tradition from your fathers; but with the precious blood of Christ, as of a lamb without blemish and without spot: who verily was foreordained before the foundation of the world, but was manifest in these last times for you" (1 Pet1:18-20.) The old hymn sums it up this way, "What can wash away my sins, nothing but the blood of Jesus; what can make me whole again, nothing but the blood of Jesus" (Lyrics and music written by Robert Lowry, 1826-1899.) Because the blood of Jesus has life eternal in it, it overcomes death and the sin which caused it. The blood is real, efficacious, all powerful, all redeeming, able to restore, sanctify, and protect from the powers of darkness. Revelation 12:11 strongly proclaims, "They overcame him [the devil] by the blood of the lamb and the word of their testimony, and they loved not their lives unto the death." The Greek word for *overcame* is *nikao* (which is where the company Nike originally got their name from) which means to conquer, prevail, get the victory. Something about the blood that separates us from the enemy of our souls; it takes away the power of the devil over our lives. It puts the devil on the run because when God sees the blood applied, that's where His manifest presence reveals His authority; and wherever God makes His authority tangible, the devil must go! In the book of Exodus, God said, "When I see the blood, I will pass over you" (Ex. 12:13.) Notice He didn't say, "When the devil sees the blood" or "when Pharoah sees the blood" or "when the Egyptians see the blood" or "when the elders of the Israel see the blood." No, God's holy and just wrath must be appeased, and only when He acknowledges the blood is peace made. This is what Christ accomplished at the cross of Calvary first and foremost: "peace with God through our Lord Jesus Christ" is what we have according to Romans 5:1. We were enemies of God until the blood made a way to be reconciled with Him. Praise be to our Lord Jesus Christ forevermore!

Certainly, what the blood of Jesus accomplished and why it is so integral to the plan of God for the redemption of man from the slave-market of sin is a mystery in part. Yes, we understand from Leviticus 17:11 that "the life of the flesh is in the blood," but we would think, "If God is God, then why couldn't He devise a less painful, gruesome way of redeeming mankind?" As Moses was travelling back to Egypt with his family after his well-known encounter with God at the burning bush, God met Moses at the inn to *kill* him because he had not circumcised his son

(Ex. 4:24.) Did you get that? God was ready to kill the man He had called up to deliver the Jews because the covenant, which is ratified by the blood of circumcision had not been kept! Zipporah, Moses wife, after performing the rite, "cut off the foreskin of her son and cast it at his [Moses'] feet and said, 'Surely a bloody husband art thou to me'" (Ex. 4:25.) Since Zipporah was a Midianite whose practice it was to circumcise a bridegroom, not a child, was taking out her frustration with Yahweh God on Moses. She couldn't take out her retaliation for her disdain for God's ways on Him directly so she blurted out her anger on Moses. This is the normal human reaction to God's blood-stained path to righteousness. It is offensive to the natural man when acknowledging the blood is the only way into His manifest presence. When David sinned in his adultery with Bathsheba, he cried, "Purge me with hyssop and I shall be clean" (Ps. 51:7.) The hyssop spoke of the blood (Heb. 9:19.) David knew none of his rationalizations or even his heartfelt regret could justify himself before God. He understood that only the application of the blood in the spirit through sincere repentance and unabridged confession of sin would restore fellowship back with God. David said, "Thou desirest not sacrifice, else I would give it; thou delightest not in burnt offering. The sacrifices of God are a broken spirit, a broken and a contrite heart, O God, thou wilt not despise" (Ps. 51:16-17.) He realized that God wanted to apply the blood to his inward man before the shedding of blood would be accepted in the outward slaying of sacrifices that were commanded. This is clear from later verses in

27

the same Psalm, "Then shalt thou be pleased with the sacrifices of righteousness, with burnt offering and whole burnt offering: then shall they offer bullocks upon thine altar" (v. 19.) Where sin is, so is death, so God takes the blood which has life in it like nothing else has. Life wipes out death to restore back to its prior estate. This is God's design.

Bringing this Old Testament example into the New Testament is what Christ has done through "the blood of the cross" (Col. 1:27.) It had to be through crucifixion that Jesus would have to die so the work of the blood would have its full effect. Notice it was not the blood of stoning or blood of a tragic fall or blood of a terrible accident or blood of assassination, but specifically **the blood of the cross** that made the provision for salvation complete. Deuteronomy 21:23, "Cursed is he that hangeth on a tree," prophesying the ignominious death Christ would suffer. The Apostle Paul confirms it in Galatians 3:13 which is another case in point where New Testament is in the Old Testament concealed and the Old Testament is in the New Testament revealed.

Jesus Christ, the Son of the Living God, became a curse so that we might receive the blessing. God the Father made Jesus, His Son, the curse so that we could be made right with God through His suffering and total, absolute shedding of His blood. It's worthwhile to note that after Jesus' resurrection and appearances to His apostles in His risen state, He did not say, "A spirit hath not flesh and blood"; rather He said, "...a spirit hath not flesh and bones" (Lk 24:39.) Why did Jesus say it that way? All of His blood had been poured out at Calvary. The Roman soldier pierced His side and ruptured His beatless heart producing an open gusher of "blood and water" (Jn. 19:34) which had not already been shed during His six grueling, anguishing hours on Calvary's tree. Thus, there was not one drop of blood that remained in His physical man. This is why Hebrews 7:16 says, "Who is made, not after the power of a carnal commandment, but after the power of an endless life." Jesus' resurrected, now glorified life has no need of physical blood to sustain it but has eternal life flowing through Him. What a divine revelation!

In considering all this, it is profound to understand that God, knowing His Son would be crucified at the hands of wicked men, would even allow the tree that would be used to execute Him to grow. Chuck Lawrence, a song writer and minister wrote a song in 1982 made famous by both Barbara Mandrell and Evangelist Jimmy Swaggart that speaks beautifully to this awesome truth. Here are some of the lyrics:

Song: "He Grew The Tree".
He molded and built such a small, lonely hill
That He knew would be called Calvary
Then He made a seed that would grow to be
The tree that would make His Son bleed
Then He made a green stem, gave it leaves
Then gave it sunshine and rain and sheltered it with moss
He grew the tree He knew would be used to make
The old rugged cross.

Nothing took His life, with love He gave it
He was crucified on a tree that He created
With great love for man, God stayed with His plan
He grew the tree He knew would be used to make
The old rugged cross.

It staggers the imagination to even consider this, but it does add up biblically speaking. Isaiah 53:10 says, "Yet it pleased the LORD [YAHWEH] to bruise him [Jesus.]" God knew the only way to forever rid mankind of sin was through sinless blood; to possess sinless blood, God needed a perfect man and the human race could not produce it on their own since all inherited sin-tainted blood from their ancestry. In the master plan of heaven, Christ agreed with the Father along with the witness of the Holy Spirit to be born in the womb of a virgin of Jewish heritage to generate the perfect man with pure, sinless blood. This was confirmed by living a perfect, sinless life ready to be offered at the quintessential moment to shed the **blood of the cross** to make provision for the redemption of mankind. No wonder the Apostle Paul proclaims boldly, "For had they [the devil and the demon powers] known it, they would not have crucified the Lord of glory" (2 Cor. 2:8.)

The blood that Jesus sacrificed at Calvary was and is *eternal* blood, meaning that it lives forever and has power. Certainly, the Bible confirms the eternal nature of the blood. Hebrews 9:12, "Neither by the blood of goats and calves, but by his own blood [of Christ] he entered in once into the holy place, having obtained eternal redemption for us." Somehow through God's supernatural operation, the blood of Jesus was transported to heaven after it was spilled out on the earth as the verse clearly states, "...by his own blood he entered in once into the holy place." This is not just a poetic note of hyperbole, but an event that actually occurred. Some scholars believe that this happened between the time Christ appeared to Mary Magdalene after His resurrection and when he showed Himself alive to the apostles in hiding. When Jesus revealed Himself to Mary after He rose from the dead, He said, "Touch me not, for I am not yet ascended to my Father; but go to my brethren, and say unto them, I ascend unto my Father and your Father; and to my God and your God" (Jn. 20:17.) Yet, later that same day, he appeared unto His apostles leaving it open for them to touch His hands and His side. No doubt, He performed His priestly duty in heaven only to return to show Himself as God and Savior to His followers.

The blood of the Savior not only has power in vibrancy, but it also speaks. Hebrews 12:24 says, "And to Jesus the mediator of the new covenant, and to the blood of sprinkling that speaketh better things that that of Abel." The blood of Abel cried out for vengeance against Cain, his brother, for murdering Abel, and justifiably so as Abel was innocent of any wrongdoing; rather, it was Cain's jealousy that caused him to kill his brother. In Genesis 4, God even so testified to Cain that "the voice of thy brother's blood crieth unto me from the ground" (v. 10.) Yes, the blood of man speaks, but the blood of Jesus speaks in the most holy of heaven even more powerfully of mercy and forgiveness. All those who humbly call out to the Savior receive the application and benefits of the precious blood of the Lamb. Thank God for the blood!

The blood that Jesus shed also has immeasurable value. All the gold, silver, precious stones, gems, land, assets of monetary value, and like-kind exchanges of worth of this world do not hold a candle to the incomprehensible price of the eternal blood of Jesus. Even added up altogether, the total tangible assets of the whole world could not buy one soul off the slave-market of sin, but the blood of the Lamb can redeem or buy back every soul that cries out to be saved from sin and its deadly consequences. Revelation 5:9 asserts emphatically, "...for thou wast slain and hast redeemed us to God by thy blood out of every kindred, and tongue, and people and nation." What a lavish Creator as well as a God of diversity! He poured out the most expensive commodity in the universe to pay the necessary price that the eternal courts of justice demanded for restoration of fellowship between God and man which had been lost in the Garden of Eden.

Truly, His blood makes even peace with God. Colossians 1:20 says, "And, having made peace through the blood of the cross, by him to reconcile all things unto himself; by him, I say all things, whether they be things in earth or things in heaven." What a statement of fullness, clarity, and conviction the Apostle Paul makes here concerning the blood. It covers all in all, and nothing is left undone whether it be in heaven or in earth. It claims absolute, unequivocal and total satisfaction to God's standard of justice and equity. Also, the blood is connected between heaven and earth as the verse implies. 1 John 5:7-8 states, "For there are three that bear record in heaven, the Father, the Word and the Holy Ghost and these three are one. And there are three that bear witness in the earth [notice, there's a record in heaven, but there's a witness in the earth] the spirit, the water and the blood and these three agree in one." The Spirit, also known as the Holy Ghost, is the connecting agent of the record in heaven and the witness in the earth. As the Spirit bears witness in the earth with the water and the blood, He speaks in heaven at the same time implicitly of that witness of the water and the blood also; so while the Holy Spirit is bearing record in heaven, He is connecting the witness of the water and the blood from earth as well, and vice versa. There's an intermingling of the record in heaven and the witness in the earth so a oneness is created with all the parties involved. The blood speaks of mercy in heaven and it proclaims Christ's Lordship in the earth. The mind of the divine cannot be fathomed.

We know also of the importance of the blood in the natural realm. The blood carries oxygen and nutrients to the physical man; it also provides clotting capability in case of cuts or internal wounds. Medical science has made great discoveries about human blood to the point that it has been able to produce certain aspects of the blood: red blood cells, white blood cells, platelets, and plasma. Yet it cannot create the blood itself which is why the Red Cross always needs blood donors. There's something in the movement and flow of human blood that gives it the unique qualities that it has, which is somewhat of a mystery indeed.

This is true as well in the spiritual realm. Just as the blood flows in the natural, so does it flow in the spiritual world. The Spirit carries the witness of the blood and water with it (1 Jn. 5:8.) Moreover, Jesus said "The wind bloweth where it listeth and you can hear the sound thereof but canst not tell from whence it cometh and whither it goeth: so is everyone that is born of the Spirit" (Jn. 3:8.) As the Spirit moves, so does the blood and the water with Him. Actually, the blood is the tangible symbol of the Spirit while the water is the symbol of the Word (Eph. 5:26.)

The Spirit and the Word are always in harmony with one another. In John 6, Jesus used the blood and the bread as symbolic of the Spirit and the Word. "Except you drink my blood and eat my flesh, you have no life in you" (v. 53.) Obviously, He was not talking about His physical flesh and blood as He sacrificed all His physical life on Calvary. Jesus was inferring that to eat His flesh was akin to feeding on His word, aka as the Word of God, or the Bible, and the blood represented the Spirit along with its power to bring life. It has been said, "The Word without the Spirit, you dry up; the Spirit without the

Word, you blow up; the Spirit and the Word, you grow up." These two dynamics work in tandem with each other and they never disagree but rather, confirm and strengthen each other in the believer's life.

We can discuss the importance of the blood further, but hopefully, you have gained enough understanding that without it, there is NO redemption, NO salvation, NO blessed hope, NO way into being a child of God. If it makes sense and you have not prayed a prayer of salvation yet, pray this from your heart:

God, I know I am a sinner; I realize that all the good works in the world cannot atone for my sins. I acknowledge your Son's sacrifice on the cross with the shedding of His blood that washes my sins away. By your grace, I repent. Save me now for Jesus' sake by the power of His blood. Thank you. Amen!

CHAPTER 4

RELIGION V. REALITY

One of the most difficult issues relative to the discussion of the reality of God and His sovereignty is the topic of religion. Religion by itself, as most understand it, acknowledges the outward appearances or trappings of some reverence towards deity. It may reflect what one might call true religion or it may just be a show of religious affections (as Jonathan Edwards spoke of) meaning a conformity to a system of teaching and practices as the Apostle Paul mentions particularly as it relates to the last days in 2 Timothy 3:5, who have a "form of godliness but deny the power thereof...". In other words, they have an understanding about God but do not know Him personally. As it has been said, "going to church does not make one a Christian any more than standing in a garage makes you a mechanic." One can believe in God and yet, not be truly a child of God. James, Jesus' half-brother says, "Thou believest in one God; thou doest well: the devils also believe, and tremble" (Jms. 2:19.) Mental assent and acknowledgment are not enough to fulfill what is necessary to be birthed into the family of God.

This grates against what most people seem to consider as sufficient religious persuasion as identifiable and acceptable before God. Man has created his own set of criteria, whether it is based originally on the Christian faith or some other religion, to attain a right-standing before God. Defined in this way, religion is man's attempt to reach God by, in essence, good works in whatever form they may be. God does not accept good works as a way to true salvation. The Jews in Jesus' day asked Him in John 6, "What shall we do, that we might work the works of God?" (v. 28.) This is man's default position: he feels he must DO something. Notice Jesus' response in v. 29, "This is the work of God, that ye believe on whom he hath sent." Religion usually focuses its attention on **doing** while true faith rests its belief on **being**: being like the one you believe on by His matchless grace.

It is interesting to note that the term *religion* is only mentioned five times in the New Testament in the KJV and only twice as it relates to the Christian faith. As it is stated in James 1:26-27, the word *religion* from the Greek is *threskeia* (Strong's Concordance #2356) meaning a ceremonial observance. This in and of itself does not save you. James 1:27 says, "Pure religion and undefiled before God and the Father is this, to visit the fatherless and widows in their affliction, and to keep himself unspotted from the world." In other words, James is saying it must be heartfelt first: *pure* is the key word and the only way for it to be truly pure is through the spiritual connection of the born-again experience. It must be religion based on relationship first. Matthew 7:21-23 speaks of those who had religion but not relationship.

Jesus speaking, "Not everyone that saith unto me, Lord, Lord shall enter into the kingdom of heaven; but he that doeth the will of my Father which is in heaven. Many will say unto me in that day, Lord, Lord have we not prophesied in thy name and in thy name, cast out devils? And in thy name done many wonderful works? And then will I profess unto them, I never knew you: depart from me, ye that work iniquity." This has to be one of the most frightful, mind-numbing, sobering passages in the entirety of the Bible. These were some of the most religious people to have ever walked the face of the earth and yet, Jesus unequivocally indicated they were not saved. They were using Jesus' name but not submitted to the authority of His name through the experiential knowledge of the cross of Christ. These men were building their own kingdom, not the kingdom of God according to the "will of my Father" (v. 21.) They were bringing glory to themselves as contrasted with Jesus' exhortation earlier in the Sermon On The Mount in Matthew 5:16, "Let your good works so shine before men, that they may see your good works and glorify your Father which is in heaven."

Jesus certainly embraced and lived this truth out each moment of His life and ministry. He took no glory for Himself but rather, glorified the Father in all that He was doing as well as teaching. John 5:30 records Jesus saying, "I can of mine own self do nothing: as I hear, I judge: and my judgment is just because I seek not mine own will, but the will of the Father which hath sent me." Another witness is John

14:10, "Believest thou not that I am in the Father and the Father in me? The words that I speak unto you I speak not of myself: but the Father that dwelleth in me, he doeth the works." A third witness is John 7:16, "My doctrine is not mine, but his that sent me." Everything that Jesus did relative to any ministry was attributed exclusively to divine origin.

While religion is only mentioned five times in the Bible as previously stated, *spirit* and *spiritual* is used over 500 times; *spiritual* is used 23 times in the New Testament predominantly in the Epistles of Paul. You can sense the emphasis is readily towards something that's living as opposed to the deadness of formality and man-made systems. Webster Dictionary defines *religion* several different ways. First, it defines it as "the service and worship of God or the supernatural as well as commitment or devotion to religious faith or observance." My sense is this is a positive take on religion. It emphasizes the focus on God and the spirit realm as opposed to what man has developed to find a way to God's Presence. The second definition it gives is "a personal set or institutionalized system of religious attitudes, beliefs and practices." This is where the human family gets in trouble regarding religion. To have a "personal or institutionalized system" based on the Word of God is acceptable and potentially productive concerning spiritual growth; however, normally when man puts his hand to add additions to what the whole counsel of God has stated as sufficient, it usually veers off-track from the tried-and-true path of truth. It can quickly descend into a system of works. This outworking of religion is a dilution and can be a deception to the essential cause of Christ which was and is to reconcile humanity back to a living, vital relationship with the Creator as it was back in the Garden of Eden. Jesus in several places made scathing denouncements against the religious rulers for their ceremonial machinations. In Matthew 23:15-16 Jesus said, "Woe unto you, scribes and Pharisees, hypocrites! For ye compass sea and land to make one proselyte, and when he is made, you make him twofold more the child of hell than yourselves. Woe unto you, ye blind guides, which say, Whosoever shall swear by the temple, it is nothing; but whosoever shall swear by the gold of the temple, he is a debtor." Jesus had a kinetic disdain for religion as we know it which produced a diametrically opposed result to the Word of God. Mark 7:9-13 records Jesus speaking to the Pharisees who were concerned about His disciples' lack of hygiene when eating bread, "Full well ye reject the commandment of God that ye may keep your own tradition. For Moses said, Honour thy father and thy mother; and whosoever curseth father or mother, let him die the death: but ye say, if a man shall say to his father or mother, it is a gift [designated to go to God relieving one of his duty to provide for his parents] by whatsoever thou mightest be profited by me; he shall be free. And ye suffer him no more to do ought for his father or mother; making the Word of God of none effect through the tradition which ye have delivered; and many such like things do ye." This is evidence that religion, at a minimum, is impotent and, even worse, dangerous. Religion can actually be used to dismiss God and His ways right out of the church and the lives caught up in it. The Lord accused the Jewish leaders of His day of displacing God and His Word with their own structure of man-made doctrine and dictates of formal behavior.

This phenomenon can truly replace reality for religion, power for politics, faith for form, and the Spirit for systems. Not surprising, as this is man's default position, to fall back into something that appeals to the soul of man as opposed to the persistent seeking for the spirit-man's connection to God. It somehow appeals, even unconsciously, to this inward disposition in man to control and determine what should constitute his own righteousness before Deity. The Apostle Paul states this well in Romans 10:3, "For they being ignorant of God's righteousness, and going about to establish their own righteousness, have not submitted themselves unto the righteousness of God."

Much of the Jewish religion by the time Jesus appeared on the scene had metastasized into a complex set of rules to follow established by the rabbis to systematize a legalistic code of behavior whereby one could justify himself before the Elders of Israel and thus, indirectly, before God. When Jesus healed on the Sabbath day, the Pharisees almost lost their minds. In John 5 (one of my favorite chapters in all of the Bible), Jesus healed a lame man at the pool of Bethesda in Jerusalem who had been in that case for thirty-eight years! But instead of rejoicing with the man, the religious leaders were upset because Jesus had performed this miracle on the Sabbath day. In fact, verse 16 says they "sought to slay him [Jesus.]" This is what religion can do: it can cause you "to strain at a gnat and swallow a camel" (Matt. 23:24); it can cause you to miss the forest for the trees; it can blind you from God Himself and His true workings.

Another case of Jesus healing on the Sabbath day occurred in John 9 when He gave a blind man sight. While the religious rulers had their rulebook, the blind man had an experience of progressive realization of who Jesus Christ really was and is. In verse 17, responding to the Pharisees questioning him as to who Jesus was, the blind man said after receiving his sight, "He is a prophet" (v. 17.) In verse 32-33, the formerly blind man comes to the conclusion that Jesus is a miracle worker: v. 32, "Since the world began was it not heard that any man opened the eyes of one that was born blind." After being thrust out of the temple for his confession by the Pharisees, Jesus found the man and revealed Himself as the Son of God (v. 35-36) which the man did receive and worshipped (v. 38.) The blind man who could now see had a dynamic progressive revelation of Jesus Christ to the saving of his soul while the Pharisees had the dead letter of their laws and traditions preventing them from entering into the vital relationship with God and the Messiah right there before them in the flesh!! Further, Jesus said in verse 41, "If ye were blind, ye should have no sin; but now ye say, 'We see;' therefore your sin remaineth." What an indictment! The ones who believed they had the code for righteousness before God were languishing in a morass of lifelessness and condemnation.

This is often the result of religion not based on a living, loving relationship with the Savior. God wants to impart life, not the dead letter of the law. Paul writes in 2 Corinthians 3:6, "...for the letter of the law killeth, but the spirit *giveth* [from the Greek, *quickeneth*] life." Jesus said in John 6:63, "...the words that I speak unto you, they are spirit and they are life." God is not interested in giving us a boring religious existence but rather, a new life. 2 Corinthians 5:17 says, "Therefore, if any man be in Christ, he is a new creature: old things are passed away; behold, all things are become new." The Amplified Bible states it this way, "Therefore, if any person is [ingrafted] in Christ [the Messiah], he is a new creation [a new creature altogether]; the old [previous moral and spiritual condition] has passed away. Behold the fresh and the new has come!" In Psalm 16:11, King David says, "...in thy presence is fulness of joy; at thy right hand, there are pleasures for evermore." What a revelation that God is into pleasure. Our God is a God of joy! "The joy of the Lord is your strength" (Neh. 8:10.) Even when Jesus was steeling Himself to endure the most excruciating ordeal in history, His crucifixion, the Bible says in Hebrews 12:2, "...who for the joy that was set before him endured the cross, despising the shame, and is set down at the right hand of the throne of God."

So, we see that while God is looking to impart life, vitality, and energy to the inner man first, man quite often desires to limit God and His flow through religion to control the effects of it on the people under their oversight. If God was to breakout like He did on the day of Pentecost in Acts 2, He might cause people to do something outside of their approved religious framework and thus, bring forth a manifestation of the Spirit which would displace the codified structure of acceptable manner and behavior. Once a man accepts certain religious ideologies over the Word of God, it becomes difficult to allow something new or fresh into that particular denomination, order, ministry, religious group or individual life. It can become a most despicable form of pride. Billy Graham once said, "There's no pride like religious pride." Saying this as respectfully as possible, but endeavoring to state the truth, religion, by itself, can take you to hell if it ultimately causes you to miss Christ in the end. This is the truth according to Jesus Himself in different places and moments. In John 5:39-40, He says, "Search the scriptures, for in them, ye think ye have eternal life; and they are they which testify of me. And you will not come unto me that ye might have life."

Pride was keeping the leaders of Jesus' day from receiving Him; and pride is a strong trait of satan. God speaking to Lucifer, satan's name in heaven, in Ezekial 28:15, "Thou wast perfect in thy ways from the day that thou was created, till iniquity was found in thee." Verse 17 says, "Thine heart was lifted up because of thy beauty, thou hast corrupted thy wisdom by reason of thy brightness: I will cast thee to the ground..." Satan's heart was lifted up, and his pride brought him down, but in going down, he is determined to take the human race with him as his way of attacking God. He knows he cannot attack God directly, so he goes after his creation; and one of his best ways to attack deceitfully is through religion. The devil is a master religionist. He cunningly devises ways for man to justify himself before God from the true way of salvation by the grace of God "through faith in his blood" (Rom. 3:25.) The devil hates the blood because he knows once the blood is applied, he can do nothing to take hold of that which has been covered and sealed by the life that's in the blood. This is true religion as opposed to man's religion which tries to work its path to God on his own merits.

Perhaps, one of the greatest examples in the Bible of a very spiritual person who confronted the religion of his day was John the Baptist. John was fearless, and relentless in addressing man-made religion and hypocrisy. In Matthew 3:7 when the Pharisees and Sadducees came out to see John baptizing, John boldly asked them, "O generation of vipers, who had warned you to flee the wrath to come? Bring forth therefore fruits meet for repentance: and think not to say within yourselves, We have Abraham to our father: for I say unto you God is able of these stones to raise up children unto Abraham. And now also the axe is laid unto the root of the trees: therefore every tree which bringeth not forth good fruit is hewn down and cast into the fire" (v. 7-10.) John had not taken any Dale Carnegie courses on *How to Win Friends and Influence People*, so you'll have to overlook his poor manners. John wanted to see heartfelt turning to God and not just a show of religious orthodoxy, hierarchy, and meritocracy. But of all the impact that John the Baptist had, nothing he did was greater than declaring that Jesus was the Messiah: "Behold the Lamb of God which taketh away the sin of the world" (Jn. 1:29.) This was a moment the world needed: to hear that the Promised One had come on the scene of history to deliver humanity from its ills, pains, sufferings hopelessness, and emptiness of existence including the machinations of ritualistic religion.

When you have the Messiah, you don't need religion as man defines it! Rituals, ceremonies, history, heritage, and liturgy based on a true, lively relationship can certainly work to enhance it; but all these efforts on their own cannot alone bridge the gulf between God and man.

Personally, I grew up in the Episcopal Church, and was confirmed with a close childhood friend of mine at 13 years old. It was a great experience, and one I will always treasure as I sensed an unusual feeling that could only be considered existential in nature, but I could not get a handle on it. Though it did not save me, God used it to help bring me to salvation years down the road. It was a spiritual experience in a religious setting, ultimately bringing me to the fuller spiritual moment later on. Religion focused on Christ as the end is a positive.

We may ask, "Did Jesus ever do religious activity?" It depends on how we define the term, but the

Bible does say, "As his custom was, he went to the synagogue on the sabbath day and stood for to read" (Lk. 4:16.) We may consider this a religious activity performed by Jesus but it had a bedrock spiritual basis. Religion can be a spiritual discipline if it has its origin in a biblically-based foundation backed by the Word of God. When He was twelve years old, His family "went up to Jerusalem after the custom of the feast" (Lk. 2:42.) Once again, it could be labeled as a religious activity but it was originally spoken by God for the Jews to observe (Deut. 16:16.) On this occasion, however, Jesus took the liberty to extend His stay at the feast and interact with the doctors of the law (Lk. 2:46); "and all that heard him were astonished at his understanding and answers" (v. 47.) His parents grieved and were relieved to find Him after three days search (v. 48), but Jesus responded, "How is it that ye sought me? Wist ye not that I must be about my Father's business?" (v. 49.) So, we see here that once the Lord had fulfilled the written dictates, He was impressed to make further inroads for His Father's kingdom by the leading of the Spirit. Later in His ministry, Jesus said, "My Father worketh hitherto and I work" (Jn. 5:17.) He followed the divine path God had given him to perform. This is not religion as the human family usually perceives it.

Frankly, religion has been a major cause or often used as a principal reason or a tool for many wars, conflicts, tensions, and deaths in human history. From the Crusades (1095-1291 apprx.) to the Muslim Jihads (particularly in the 7th-9th centuries) to The Thirty Year

War in Europe (predominantly between Catholics and Protestants from 1618-48) to the Taiping Rebellion in China in the 1800s where millions died (some estimates over 20 million) to what is known as The First Sudanese Civil War (1955-72), religion has been part and parcel of the dynamic of fightings among different people groups.

Certainly, the Bible makes place for war. Ecclesiastes says, "A time to love, a time to hate, and a time for war" (Ecc. 3:8, ESV.) Exodus 3:15 states, "The LORD is a man of war, the LORD [Yahweh] is his name." The problem is that man in his sinful state takes it too far and begins to kill, maim, and violate innocent people who are in the wrong place at the wrong time. Then, we also see blatant persecution of those affiliated with certain religious labels whether it be the feeding of Christians to the lions as in the days of Nero ruling the Roman Empire or the oppression of Muslims by the Meccans in the early days of Islam or the unfathomable torture of Jews in the Spanish Inquisition by the so-called Christian organized church. This is what religion can lead to if not led by the Holy Spirit.

Perhaps, the biggest elephant in the room concerning religious oppression is Antisemitism. Dr. MLK, Jr. said, "Antisemitism, the hatred of the Jewish people has been and remains a blot on the soul of mankind. In this, we are in full agreement. So, know also this: that anti-Zionist is inherently antisemitic and ever will be so." The oldest form of racism in the world is antisemitism and seems to ebb and flow from generation to generation. From Haman to

Hitler (6 million+ Jews exterminated in the Holocaust) to Hussein (Sadam) to Hamas and Hezbollah, there seems to be a connecting thread: a spirit of hatred against the Jewish people gets passed down through the eons of time because of jealousy and envy. As God called them His Chosen People (Deut. 7:6; Is. 43:4; Rom. 11:29), the devil has inspired hatred of the Jews through different leaders and people groups as retaliation for their perceived elevated status before the Creator. The problem for the Jewish people is that when you are chosen, more is expected of you and when this was not fulfilled, more negative consequences resulted. Luke 12:48 says, "For unto whomsoever much is given, of him shall be much required."

The Jews were given everything that related to the first covenant: the law, in particular, the Ten Commandments, the tabernacle, the sacrifices, the glory, and most of all, the promised Messiah. The rest of the world developed a deep-seated jealousy over the generations against them for God's sovereign election and has tried to wipe them out or, at a minimum, push them out of whatever land they possessed. It became a target on their back to the point that even Jesus wept over Jerusalem for their blindness over missing their "time of visitation" to receive God's salvation (Lk. 19:41-44.)

What the world fails to recognize is that once one accepts the Jewish Messiah as Savior, they become a chosen one. In fact, once the born-again experience happens, that individual has much greater intimacy with God than a natural Jew who is

49

not saved. The book of Hebrews makes the case thoroughly that the new covenant which was cut by Jesus Christ at the cross of Calvary is much better and more powerful than the first covenant featuring the law. This greater revelation for Jew and Gentile alike has also become a target on the backs of those who claim it. There is a price to claim God as your Father and Jesus Christ as the only Savior of the world. 1 Timothy 2:5 clearly states, "For there is one God and one mediator between God and men, the man Christ Jesus." This is an offense to the pluralistic thinking and worldview of universal society.

In summary, religion alone has not delivered man from his sinful state because "Ye must be born again." Jesus did not leave heaven and the glory He had with the Father to come to earth to start a new religion. A thousand times, NO! He came to fulfill the law given through Moses (Matt. 5:17-18) and to establish a better covenant. This better covenant brought forth a new relationship between God and His creation, that of Fatherhood and children through the complete satisfactory work of Christ on Calvary's cruel cross to make provision for full salvation and intimate relations with God Almighty.

If you believe with all your heart that Christ and only Christ can save you, pray this out loud. God will bless your faith to speak it:

"God, I know I am a sinner; I need Jesus to save me from my sins. O, God, save me now for Jesus' sake. Thank you. Amen!"

CHAPTER 5
CONCLUDING THOUGHTS

The purpose of this short book is not to condemn anybody's particular beliefs, but rather to challenge those beliefs to see if they align with the plumbline of the Word of God. If you are an atheist or agnostic and you have gotten this far in reading, I commend you. I don't blame you for your position. With all the pain and evil in this world, it's understandable. One has to wonder though, how and why are we here? Dionne Warwick sang that famous song so beautifully back in the sixties, "What's It All About, Alfie?" questioning the point of existence without love. If that's true, where does love come from, anyway? There has to be a source; there has to be a Creator.

Our Founding Fathers certainly believed that. The opening line of the Declaration of Independence leaves no doubt, "We hold these truths to be self-evident that all men are created equal; that they are endowed by their Creator with certain unalienable rights that among these are life, liberty and the pursuit of happiness." Pres. JFK in his inaugural speech on Jan. 20, 1961, said, "And yet the same revolutionary beliefs for which our forbears fought are still at issue around the globe – the belief that the rights of man come not from the generosity of the state, but from the hand of God."

God Himself does not try to make a case for His existence in the Bible. In the very first verse, Moses states, as a matter of fact, "In the beginning, God made the heavens and the earth" (Gen. 1:1.) The Almighty does not come out begging for anyone to believe in Him. He just explains how everything was made and we have the right to accept it or reject it. In the original Hebrew, the word for *created* is *bara* which means made out of nothing. It is reserved for God alone as only He can bring something into existence to the material realm into the tangible world. The Latin expression often used is *ex nihilo*.

This whole theory of the Big Bang is implausible as it breaks the law of non-contradiction which disallows a statement and its negation to be true at the same time and in the same sense. To say that order (of nature and its expanse in this case) came out of disorder is a contradiction in terms. It would be akin to saying a beautiful, perfectly painted, precision-running, stellar, candy-red Cadillac was produced by a tornado blowing through a junkyard. It didn't happen and neither did it happen for the universe. Rest assured, it's all here by design.

Genesis 1:1 also covers the five key attributes of natural phenomena promoted by a 19th century philosopher, Herbert Spencer, who was considered an agnostic. "In the beginning [time], God [force] created [action] the heavens [space] and the earth [matter.] These five basic principles, time, force, action, space, and matter are the foundational explanation of why anything existing exists. The Psalmist declares in affirmation, "The heavens declare the glory of God and the firmament showeth his handywork. Day unto day uttereth speech, night unto night sheweth knowledge. There is no speech nor language where their voice is not heard" (Ps. 19:1-3.) Nature declares the incontrovertible being of God.

This is one of the seven revelations that God has presented in the earth and human history, as stated in Thompson Chain Reference Bible (Ref. #4219.) It shows these Seven Editions of Divine Law as follows:

- Written on nature (Ps. 19:1)
- Written on conscience (Rom. 2:15)
- Written on Tables of Stone (Ex. 24:12)
- The entire scriptures (Rom. 15:4)
- Christ, the Illustrated Edition (Jn. 1:14)
- Written on the heart (Heb. 8:10)
- The outward Christian life: living epistles (2 Cor. 3:2-3)

Perhaps the 7th edition may be the most difficult to accept because God is working this reality out through very imperfect people and this makes it even more astonishing because He can still ultimately bring forth His will through such. As I share with others sometimes, "If you ever find a perfect church, please do not walk in there; because the moment you walk in there, it will no longer be perfect." Although we are all imperfect, we have a perfect God (Ps. 18:30) who always has a solution to our questions and our problems.

Of course, if one denies the Bible as the Word of God, it is difficult to accept this foundational assertion of divine revelation. It is worthy to consider, though, that only three major texts claim to be the Word of God: the Bible, the Koran, and the Book of Mormon (the Hindu religion has writings claiming to be of divine origins, but not a major text.) They cannot all be the Word of God as they do contradict each other in different ways. The Bible claims to be the final, authoritative, inherent, infallible written Word of God for the human family. We must remember that the Koran was written by Mohammed who was not even born until the 6th century and the Book of Mormon not until the 1800s. All the New Testament books were written by **eyewitnessess** of Jesus, including Paul's epistles as he met Jesus personally on the road to Damascus (Acts 9.) Neither Mohammed or Joseph Smith can say they were eyewitnesses to Jesus Christ. They certainly could have had an experience of some sort but none that equal the Bible that was already in place and readily accepted as the final Word of God. The Koran even states in 5:46-47 its belief in the Torah and the Gospel and Jesus Himself. The main difference is that it does not affirm Christ's deity on which the Bible makes no equivocation.

The Bible's 66 books have stood the test of time over and over, even when the Catholic Church has canonized 73 at the Council of Trent in 1546 to distinguish itself from The Reformation Movement.

YE MUST BE BORN AGAIN

Nonetheless, both the Catholic and the Protestant Churches agree on the main 66 books as being canon-worthy through much scrutiny, study, and steadfastness. Other books were deemed helpful but not canon-worthy. God directed the process by divine providence. The Apostle John warns against adding to or taking away from the accepted Word of God (Rev. 22:18-19.) The Holy Spirit will give anyone that truly desires to know the truth an inner witness to which book is ultimately *the* Truth, not just *a* truth. Jesus said, "Everyone who is of the truth heareth my voice" (Jn. 18:37.)

There must be something to the Bible as approximately 100 million bibles of different versions and languages are sold each year. Wikipedia states, "The Bible is considered the best-selling book of all time." Why is that? Because it is a living book. You don't read the Bible as much as it reads you! Hebrews 4:12 says, "For the Word of God is quick and powerful and sharper than any two-edged sword piercing to the dividing asunder of soul and spirit and of the joints and marrow, and is a discerner of the thoughts and intents of the heart." In the original Greek, the *word* is *logos* (Strong's Concordance #3056) mentioned previously as meaning the entire thought or divine expression. The written Word becomes the spoken Word and the living Word which is Christ Himself who gives life; and by his Spirit, He anoints the written and spoken Word powerfully.

We know that for a fact because when Jesus was in the wilderness, He said to the devil, "It is written" (Matt. Chapter 4.) The living Word spoke the written

Word (Gr. *logos*) to become the spoken Word (Gr. *Rhema.*) In other words, it became a quickened Word, an utterance which has authority in the spiritual realm. When Jesus had said, "It is written" upon His third major test in the wilderness with the devil in Matthew 4, it says, "Then the devil leaveth him and, behold, angels came and ministered unto him" (v. 11.) Proverbs 18:21 records, "Death and life are in the power of the tongue." Jesus proved Himself as having total, unequivocal authority over satan and the powers of evil. Whatever He commanded them to do, they obeyed.

In the final analysis, Jesus is either a liar, a lunatic, or He is Lord. No man could make the claims which He claimed about Himself unless He is lying, out of His right mind, or Lord as He claimed. The "I AM" statements He proclaims in the Gospel of John clearly show Jesus believed and knew that He was and is God in the flesh. He said, "I am the way, the truth and the life" (Jn. 14:6); "I am the door" (Jn. 10:9); "Before Abraham was, I am" (Jn. 8:58); upon gathering the Pharisees to arrest Jesus in the Garden of Gethsemane, He said, "I am (he)" and they fell backward from the power of His claim (Jn. 18:5.) The word *he* in the KJV is in *italics* to show it was not in the original Greek but was put in by the translators for context. This was a clear inference to Moses' encounter with the burning bush on the backside of a mountain where He revealed Himself as "I AM THAT I AM" (Ex. 3:14.) Scholars are not exactly sure as to how to precisely interpret God's revelation as what His name is except that, without exception, He is the Uncaused One. He needs nothing outside of Himself to exist; He has no beginning or end; He is always in ultimate charge; He is because He is! All this, Christ claimed about Himself. You have to accept it or reject it. Jesus never makes excuses or backs down from His claim of deity and universal authority. Matthew 28:18 says, "All power (Gr. *exousia*: authority) is given unto me in heaven and in earth."

God is omniscient (all-knowing), omnipresent (everywhere at the same time), and omnipotent (all powerful.) Jesus affirmed this about Himself. Of course, in His humanity, He was only one place at a time, but through the Holy Spirit which is the Spirit of Christ, He's everywhere. No one else can make that claim. He leaves no doubt as to who He is according to the Word of God. The Apostle Paul boldly states of Jesus that, "And without controversy, great is the mystery of godliness: God was manifest in the flesh, justified in the spirit, seen of angels, preached unto the Gentiles, believed on in this world, received up into glory" (1 Tim. 3:16.) That about summarizes it all. Jesus Christ, God Almighty in the flesh (now glorified), accomplished a mission no one else could accomplish; was victorious over all the powers of darkness and evil (Col. 2:14-15); pleased the Father in all He did; has been accepted by many down through the centuries as Savior, Lord, Master and King; and soon, is predicted to return in the not too soon distant future.

Time is coming to a close. James 4:14 says, "Whereas ye know not what shall be on the morrow. For what is your life? It is even a vapour, that appeareth for a little time and then vanisheth away." His coming is nigh at the door and each life will stand before the judgment bar of God. Hebrews 9:27-28 states, "And as it is appointed unto men once to die, but after this, the judgment: so Christ was once offered to bear the sins of many; and unto them that look for him shall he appear the second time without sin unto salvation." Most people plan more for their two-week vacation than eternity; eternity is a lot longer than two weeks. Take time to plan for eternity. Make sure your bags are packed with Jesus Christ and His full salvation.

This salvation is a very comprehensive term as well as something that we experience. If we have received Christ as Savior, then we have been saved from the penalty of sin, we are being saved from the power of sin as we submit ourselves to Him, and we will be saved from the presence of sin. God's got it covered from A to Z, and He has left nothing to chance.

Yet, with all that God has done, many are still unsure. Though there are many possible intellectual questions, I believe there are two main reasons for uncertainty about salvation. First, many people just cannot seem to admit to the fact that they are sinners. They will admit they have faults, failures, foibles, and flaws but will not admit to themselves or to God (though they probably know it in their hearts) to say, "I am a sinner." If one admits that essential truth, then by definition, he or she would realize their need for a Savior. The Apostle John said, "If we say that we have no sin, we deceive ourselves, and the truth is not in us" (1 Jn. 1:8.) He spells it out pretty plainly.

Second, if one can admit their sinful state, many cannot come to the conclusion that Jesus Christ is God Almighty. Many thousands of men were crucified on a cross during Roman rule, but their sufferings and deaths could not save one person from the penalty of sin. God had to send Himself to die for others. Certainly, we have offered Bible scriptures and evidence that Jesus was and is the Christ and God as well. However, I believe one of the greatest witnesses to the deity of Christ was the centurion who oversaw His crucifixion. A centurion was a Roman officer who had experienced much bloodshed and death during his tenure in the Roman military. They were known for their "strength, discipline and leadership"(Google.) These men were tough, callous to pain, and numb to the sensitivity of suffering. I picture a centurion as five Jack Dempseys and five Mohammed Alis all wrapped into one man. When the centurion watched Jesus on the cross and sensed the earthquake which occurred during the crucifixion, he said boldly, "Truly this was the Son of God" (Matt. 27:54.) What a powerful testimony! Wow! The man who supervised the crucifixion of Christ declared Jesus was the "Son of God!" If that doesn't grip your mind and heart, I'm not sure what will. "I know that whatsoever God doeth, it shall be forever: nothing can be put to it, nor anything taken from it: and God doeth it that men should fear before him"

(Ecc. 3:14.) If we see Christ on the cross as the Father views the moment in history, a holy fear would bring us under "the influence of divine power and persuasion" as I heard one preacher say, to humble ourselves before Him.

I will close this prose with this final thought: *One Solitary Life*

> He was born in an obscure village. He worked in a carpenter shop until he was thirty years old. He then became an itinerant preacher. He never held an office. He never had a family or owned a home. He didn't go to college. He had no credentials but Himself. He was only thirty-three when the tide of public opinion turned against Him. His friends ran away. He was turned over to His enemies and went through the mockery of a trial. He was nailed to a cross between two thieves. While He was dying, His executioners gambled for His clothing, the only property He had left on earth. He was laid in a borrowed grave.
>
> Twenty centuries have come and gone and today, He is the central figure of the human race. All the armies that have ever marched, all the navies that ever sailed, all the parliaments that ever sat, and all the kings that ever reigned have not affected life of man on this earth as much as that *One Solitary Life*.

I don't know about you, but that is someone that I want to get my wagon hitched to without delay. God bless you in your search for Truth.

ABOUT THE AUTHOR

Thomas J. Murphy is a lay preacher who has a passion to see souls come to Christ and be strengthened in the Word of God. By profession, he has worked in Executive Search and authored a booklet called *Dynamic Interviewing*. Along with his late wife, Thomas has done missionary work in Russia and two tours of Israel. He currently pastors a small Pentecostal Church in central Maryland.

ABOUT MANIFEST PUBLICATIONS

Manifest Publications is the publishing division of Manifest International, LLC. Our objective is to help like-minded ministries and writers produce and distribute materials which proclaim Jesus Christ to all the world and equip the global Church for unity and maturity.

MANIFEST
PUBLICATIONS

www.manifestinternational.com